P9-ASB-983

EXPERIMENT
WITH WEATHER

Written by Miranda Bower

Science Consultant: Bob Aran, London Weather Center

Education Consultant: Ruth Bessant

Lerner Publications Company
Minneapolis, Minnesota

All words marked in **bold** can be found in the glossary that begins on page 30.

This edition published in 1994 by:
Lerner Publications Company
241 First Avenue North
Minneapolis, Minnesota 55401

Illustration and design copyright © Two-Can Publishing Ltd, 1992
Text and compilation copyright © Miranda Bower, 1992

First published in Great Britain in 1992 by:
Two-Can Publishing Ltd.
346 Old Street
London EC1V 9NQ

Library of Congress Cataloging-in-Publication Data

Bower, Miranda.
    Experiment with weather / written by Miranda Bower.
        p.   cm.
    "First published in 1992 by Two-Can Pub. Ltd."—T.p. verso.
    Includes index.
    Summary: Provides an introduction to meteorological phenomena and includes
experiments describing various aspects of our weather, such as clouds, wind, fog,
and rainbows.
    ISBN 0-8225-2458-9
    1. Weather—Juvenile literature. 2. Weather—Experiments—Juvenile literature.
3. Meteorology—Juvenile literature. [1. Meteorology. 2. Weather—Experiments.
3. Experiments.] I. Title.
QC981.3.B7   1994
551.5'078—dc20   92-41126
                                                                    CIP
                                                                    AC

Printed in Hong Kong
Bound in the United States of America

1 2 3 4 5 6 99 98 97 96 95 94

ISBN: 0-8225-2458-9

Photographs reproduced with permission of Bruce Coleman Limited: pp. 4 left (Flip
de Nooyer), 5 top, 10, 12 (Norbert Rosing), 20 bottom, 22 bottom (John Shaw), 25 top
(David Davies), 23 top (Steve Davey); Frank Lane Picture Agency: p. 18 bottom
(R. Bird); NHPA: p. 15 top (Martin Wendler); Oxford Scientific Films: pp. 18 top
(Warren Faidley), 13, 20 top (Stan Osolinski), 14 top (Ronald Toms), 25 top (Paul
Franklin); Planet Earth Pictures: p. 14 bottom (Mark Mattack); Science Photo
Library: pp. 6 left (Dr. Fred Espenak), 11/12 background (John Mead), 27 bottom
right (Peter Menzel); Science Photo Library/European Space Agency: p. 6 left; ZEFA:
pp. 21 top, 5 left, 9 (Art Wolfe), 10 (Wienke), 16 (Photri), 28 bottom right (R. Lincks),
29 bottom left (Damm), 29 top left (Ernst A. Weber).

All other photographs by Paul Bricknell.
Illustrations by Nancy Anderson.

CONTENTS

SKY CYCLE

What is the **weather** like today? Cold and wet? Warm and sunny? Weather affects us in many ways—what we wear, how we travel, and what we do for fun.

▶ The world is divided into different **climate** zones. Tropical climates, near the **equator**, usually have hot, wet weather. Temperate climates are cold in winter and warm in summer. Polar climates have cold weather all year round.

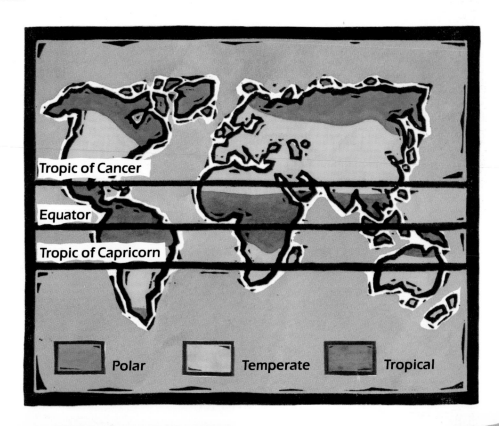

Tropic of Cancer

Equator

Tropic of Capricorn

Polar   Temperate   Tropical

▲ The Sun heats some regions on Earth more than others. Regions between the Tropic of Cancer and the Tropic of Capricorn receive a lot of heat from the Sun. The North and South poles don't receive as much sunlight.

Meteorology is the science of weather. The word comes from the Greek word *meteoron*, which means "strange event in the sky." One strange event sometimes seen in the night sky is the **aurora**, flashes of light occurring near the North and South poles.

The warmth of the Sun lifts water into the air from oceans, lakes, and rivers. Water in the air creates rain, fog, and snow. How do you protect yourself during wet weather?

Air that is heated by the Sun becomes lighter and rises. Cooler, heavier air rushes in to take the place of rising air. Moving air is called wind. The strongest winds on Earth blow during **hurricanes**. Hurricane winds can reach speeds of more than 150 miles per hour!

WEATHER WATCH

Did you hear the weather **forecast** today? How does a forecaster predict the weather? Forecasters study wind, rain, clouds, and **temperature** at weather stations around the world. Then the forecasters create maps showing where rain showers and snowstorms are likely to form. Computers help forecasters predict how the weather might change.

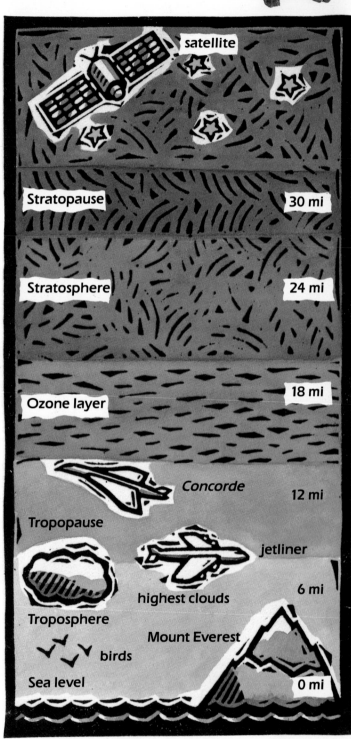

Stratopause · 30 mi

Stratosphere · 24 mi

Ozone layer · 18 mi

Concorde · 12 mi

Tropopause · jetliner

highest clouds · 6 mi

Troposphere

Mount Everest

birds

Sea level · 0 mi

▲ The computer image above shows a hurricane seen from space. The picture was created by a **satellite**, a spacecraft traveling high above the Earth.

▲ The **atmosphere** is a layer of gases surrounding the Earth. The atmosphere is divided into several regions, including the **ozone layer**. Weather develops in the **troposphere**, the part of the atmosphere nearest the ground.

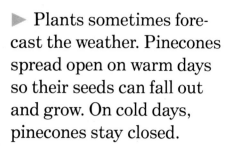

► Plants sometimes forecast the weather. Pinecones spread open on warm days so their seeds can fall out and grow. On cold days, pinecones stay closed.

▼ Satellites traveling around the Earth take photographs of clouds. Satellite photographs help scientists learn where clouds are moving, how big they are, and what kind of weather the clouds will bring.

▲ Weather balloons carry scientific instruments into the air. The instruments measure weather conditions high in the atmosphere and send information back to Earth using radio signals.

▼ If you ever visit the ocean, bring home some seaweed. Put a piece of seaweed near a door or window. When rain is coming, the seaweed will grow damp and limp. In dry weather, the seaweed will become crispy.

WATER IN THE AIR

If you hang out wet clothes on a warm, breezy day, before long your clothes will dry. The Sun's heat **evaporates** the water in the clothes, changing it into an invisible gas called **water vapor**. Air always contains water vapor, even in dry regions.

Farmers in dry parts of Australia collect rainwater in open tanks and cover the surface of the water with white plastic balls. The white balls deflect the Sun's rays, so less of the precious water evaporates.

Pour equal amounts of water into two identical containers. Put Styrofoam beads in one container and leave both containers outside in a sunny spot, protected from the wind. After several days, measure the water in each container. Which holds more water? Where did the water go?

On cold nights, water vapor **condenses**—turns from gas back into liquid water droplets. The droplets, called **dew**, cling to plants and windowpanes. Water vapor that condenses high in the air forms clouds.

CLOUDY SKIES

Clouds are made up of tiny water droplets and ice crystals floating in the air. A blue sky with puffy, white **cumulus clouds** signals fair weather. But if cumulus clouds cover most of the sky, rain showers might be coming.

▲ Fog is a cloud lying close to the ground. Fog often forms on still, cool mornings.

▼ You can make a cloud in a bottle. Ask an adult to fill a jar with hot water. Pour some of the hot water out and cover the jar with a piece of plastic wrap. Put ice cubes on top of the plastic. Water vapor will condense where the warm and cold air meet. A cloud will form in the jar.

▲ **Cumulonimbus clouds** bring thunderstorms.

▲ **Cirrus clouds** are wispy white clouds seen high in the sky.

▲ Thick, flat **stratus clouds** often bring drizzle and gloomy weather.

RAINY DAYS

Rain is part of the Earth's **water cycle**. Rain falls to the ground and collects in rivers, lakes, and oceans. The Sun's heat turns some of the water into water vapor, which rises into the sky. The water vapor cools and condenses, forming clouds. Rain falls from the clouds to Earth. The water cycle continues.

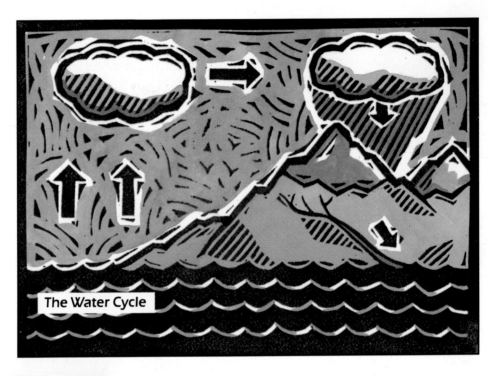

The Water Cycle

▲ Sometimes tiny water droplets in a cloud bump into each other, combine, and form raindrops. When the drops become too heavy to float in the air, they fall to the ground as rain.

▼ Fill a jar with water and set it on a sunny windowsill. Put a piece of white paper on a table beside the jar. Slide the paper around the table until bright colors appear on the paper. You've made a **rainbow**.

If rain falls when the Sun is shining, the raindrops may split the Sun's light into an arc of colors called a rainbow. Rainbows are made of red, orange, yellow, green, blue, and violet light.

FLOODWATERS

Floods are often caused by heavy rains. Rivers can swell during rainstorms and overflow their banks. Water floods the surrounding land.

► Sometimes people flood valleys on purpose by building a **dam** across a river. The water that collects behind the dam can be piped to farms and cities. Small holes in the dam let some water rush out. The rushing water turns giant blades that generate power.

◄ A sudden flood can destroy homes, kill animals and people, and ruin crops. Some places suffer from flooding every few years.

► Make a gauge to measure how much rain falls where you live. Fit a funnel into the neck of a jar and put the jar outside. Each week, pour the rainwater that collects into a measuring cup. Keep track of how much rain has fallen.

Floods aren't always disasters. In many places, such as this farm in Brazil, rivers overflow their banks each year. The water carries bits of rock called **minerals** from the riverbed to the surrounding land. After the water drains back into the river, the land is covered with mineral-rich soil, excellent for growing crops.

HOWLING WINDS

Sometimes the wind just gently flutters leaves on trees. Other times the wind blows up a storm.

▼ A **tornado** forms when a column of hot, rising air begins to spin. The tornado drops from the sky and races across the land, destroying trees, cars, and buildings.

Warm Front

Cold Front

◀ Air can be cold, warm, damp, or dry. Air near a tropical sea is often warm and wet. Air from the North Pole is usually cold and dry. A **front** is a boundary where cold air and warm air meet. Clouds and rain often form along fronts.

▶ In 1805, Sir Francis Beaufort invented a scale to measure wind speed at sea. Today Beaufort's scale is used to measure wind speed on land.

◀ To make a **weather vane**, tape paper arrows to the ends of a straw. Pin the straw into the eraser of a pencil so that the straw can spin around. Put the pencil into the bottom of an empty yogurt container.

Set the container outside and fix it in place with modeling clay.

▶ Mark north, south, east, and west on the container according to the directions shown on a compass. The arrows on your weather vane will point in the direction the wind blows.

THE BEAUFORT SCALE

0 **Calm**

1 **Light air:** Weather vanes don't move, smoke drifts with air

2 **Light breeze:** Wind felt on face, weather vanes move, leaves rustle

3 **Gentle breeze:** Leaves and twigs move, flags extend

4 **Moderate breeze:** Small branches sway, dust and paper blow about

5 **Fresh breeze:** Small trees sway, small waves form on water

6 **Strong breeze:** Large branches sway, difficult to use umbrella

7 **Moderate gale:** Large trees sway, walking against wind is difficult

8 **Fresh gale:** Twigs snap off trees

9 **Strong gale:** Shingles blow off roofs

10 **Whole gale:** Trees uprooted, damage to buildings

11 **Storm:** Widespread damage

12 **Hurricane:** Violent destruction

THUNDER AND LIGHTNING

Weather forecasters tell people if thunderstorms are likely to form where they live. Thunderstorms bring heavy rains, strong winds, and **lightning**. Thunder is the sound created by a lightning flash.

▼ Lightning can start fires and split tree trunks. This tree was struck by lightning.

▲ Lightning is a giant spark of **electricity** caused by a buildup of electrical charges within a thunderstorm. Lightning often travels from a cloud to the ground. Lightning tends to strike tall objects on the ground, like trees and buildings.

▶ Many buildings are fitted with a **lightning rod**. Lightning travels through the rod to the ground—without damaging the building.

Electricity doesn't just create lightning. You can see electricity in action in many places. Rub a balloon on your clothes and press the balloon against a smooth wall. A force called **static electricity** will make the balloon cling to the wall.

SNOW AND ICE

Inside clouds, water vapor sometimes freezes into tiny ice crystals. The crystals bump into each other and combine to become snowflakes. When the snowflakes become too heavy to float in air, they fall to the ground.

▲ **Hailstones** form when raindrops freeze inside cumulonimbus clouds and turn into solid balls of ice. The balls fall to Earth as hail. The biggest hailstone ever found was the size of an orange.

▲ When water vapor condenses on a very cold day, tiny ice crystals appear on plants and windowpanes. The ice is called **frost**.

◄ The next time snow falls, look at some snowflakes through a magnifying glass. Each snowflake has six sides. Some snowflakes are simple, others are more elaborate.

Sheep grow a thick coat of wool to protect them from the cold. In the spring, as the air gets warmer, the sheep no longer need these coats. Farmers shear the sheep, and people use the wool to make clothing.

Do not use a glass bottle. It might burst!

Fill a plastic bottle to the brim with water. Screw the lid on tightly and put the bottle in the freezer. After a while, the sides of the bottle will bulge and crack. Water expands when it freezes. On very cold days, water might freeze inside the pipes that run through your house.

HEAT AND DROUGHT

Droughts are periods when little rain falls in a region. During a drought, water supplies run low, and crops, animals, and even people might die. Soil might turn to dust and blow away.

▶ The world's **desert** regions are dry almost all year round. During some years, most of the rain that falls in a desert comes from a single downpour. An **oasis** is a fertile place in the middle of a desert.

◀ Some desert plants store scarce water in their stems and leaves.

▶ A **sundial** is a clock that uses shadows to mark the time. To make a sundial, cut out a large circle of cardboard. Cut a cardboard triangle with a flap along one side and glue the triangle onto the circle.

Set your sundial outdoors with the triangle pointing north. Each hour, mark the time of day where the Sun casts a shadow on the circle. You can use the sundial like a clock to tell time every day.

◀ Airplanes often fly above cloud level. The sky is always clear above the clouds, even if rain is falling below.

▶ A **thermometer** is a device that measures temperature. Liquid stored at the bottom of the thermometer expands in warm weather and rises. The level the liquid reaches on the thermometer shows the temperature.

Brannan
England
°C   °F
50 :: 120
40 :: 100
30 :: 80
20 :: 60
10 :: 40
0
:: 20
x 0

CHANGING WEATHER

Climates on Earth change very slowly. But some scientists think that human activity is causing climates to change more quickly.

▼ The atmosphere contains a gas called **carbon dioxide** that traps heat near the Earth. Carbon dioxide helps keep the Earth warm.

Trees use carbon dioxide to make food. But, to create farmland, people have burned large **rain forests** on Earth. Burning trees releases carbon dioxide into the air. And with fewer trees to absorb the gas, even more carbon dioxide fills the air. The extra carbon dioxide changes the balance of gases in the atmosphere, causing weather and climate to change too.

Life on Earth is affected by **air pollution.** Cars, factories, and power stations all release gases that pollute the air. The gases mix with raindrops inside clouds, creating **acid rain.** Acid rain poisons rivers and lakes. It kills trees and fish and even eats away at the sculptures and stonework on buildings.

How acid is your water? Cook a red cabbage in boiling water. Ask an adult to help you. Turn off the heat and let the cabbage sit in the water for several hours. Strain the cabbage water into a dish.

Soak strips of white coffee filter paper in the cabbage water and let the strips dry. Dip one strip into lemon juice, another into tap water, and another into rainwater. The stronger the acid in the liquid, the redder your test strip will become.

SIMPLE SEASONS

Have you ever wondered why the **seasons** change? Why do we have winter, spring, summer, and fall?

Summer in the Northern Hemisphere

Winter in the Northern Hemisphere

▲ The Earth circles the Sun once per year. As the Earth travels, different parts of the globe tilt toward the Sun at different times.

When your region leans away from the Sun, winter occurs where you live. In summer, your region tilts toward the Sun. Fall and spring are the seasons in between—when the weather becomes colder or warmer.

▼ Some animals travel to warm regions before winter arrives. These monarch butterflies fly 1,800 miles each year from North to South America.

◀ People also change their habits with the seasons. In winter we wear many layers of clothing to trap heat. In summer we wear loose clothing to keep cool. We also wear lotion and sunglasses to protect ourselves from the Sun's rays.

27

THE WEATHER AND YOU

The weather affects us in many ways. Sunny, warm weather usually makes people happy. People like to have picnics, take walks, and play outdoors on sunny days.

▼ On summer days, **pollen**, dusty spores from plants, blows around with the wind. Pollen sometimes makes people sneeze.

▲ We play different sports during different seasons. Football is a fall sport. Swimming is usually done in summer.

▲ Many people enjoy winter sports, such as skiing.

The weather affects how people live. Houses in hot countries, such as Greece, are often painted white because white surfaces reflect heat. The houses have small windows that don't let in much sunlight.

In cold countries, people put thick **insulation** in the walls of their houses to help keep the heat in.

Windy, stormy weather can make you grumpy. Many people get sick with colds and the flu during bad weather.

GLOSSARY

acid rain: rain that contains pollution

air pollution: gases, chemicals, and other impurities released into the air

atmosphere: the layer of gases surrounding the Earth

aurora: flashing lights in the sky, occurring near the North and South poles

carbon dioxide: one of many gases found in the atmosphere

cirrus cloud: a wispy, white cloud forming high in the sky

climate: the most typical weather found in a certain region on Earth

condense: to turn from gas into liquid

cumulonimbus cloud: a giant cloud that brings a thunderstorm

cumulus cloud: a puffy white cloud, common in summer

dam: a barrier built across a river

desert: a region on Earth where very little rain falls

dew: tiny water drops that form when water vapor condenses near the ground

drought: a period when little or no rain falls in a region

electricity: an energy source that provides power, heat, and light

equator: an imaginary line around the Earth, halfway between the North and South poles

evaporate: to turn from liquid into gas by heating

flood: a rising or overflowing body of water

forecast: a prediction about the upcoming weather

front: a boundary between a cold air mass and a warm air mass

frost: tiny ice crystals that form when water vapor condenses near the ground and freezes

hailstones: solid balls of ice that fall during thunderstorms

hurricane: a giant swirling storm that brings rain and destructive winds

insulation: material such as fiberglass that keeps heat from escaping through walls

lightning: a giant electrical spark created during a thunderstorm

lightning rod: a metal pole that protects buildings from lightning damage

meteorology: the study of weather

minerals: rocklike substances including salt, sand, coal, and stone

oasis: a fertile place in the middle of a desert

ozone layer: the region of the atmosphere that absorbs harmful rays from the Sun

pollen: dusty spores given off by plants

rainbow: an arc of colors created when sunlight shines through raindrops

rain forest: a lush forest found in a tropical region

satellite: a craft that orbits the Earth and assists in weather forecasting

seasons: the four periods of the year—spring, summer, winter, and fall—marked by a certain kind of weather

static electricity: a form of electricity that doesn't provide power

stratus clouds: thick, gray clouds that often bring rain

sundial: a device for telling time using shadows

temperature: a measurement of heat

thermometer: an instrument for measuring temperature

tornado: a swirling column of air that descends from a cloud to the ground

troposphere: the layer of the atmosphere nearest the Earth

water cycle: the movement of water between the Earth and the atmosphere

water vapor: water in gas form

weather: the condition of the atmosphere at a certain time and place

weather vane: a device that points in the direction of the wind

INDEX